# SKY HARBOR

# SKY HARBOR

POEMS BY

# MILES WAGGENER

PINYON PUBLISHING

Montrose, Colorado

First Edition: June 2011

Pinyon Publishing
23847 V66 Trail, Montrose, CO 81403
www.pinyon-publishing.com

Library of Congress Control Number: 2011922393
ISBN: 978-1-936671-01-4

# ACKNOWLEDGEMENTS

Portions of *Sky Harbor* have appeared in the following publications:

*Antioch Review*: "Fathers"

*Beloit Poetry Journal*: "Door" (p. 10); "Portents Aside"

*Blue Mesa Review*: "Heartland Index"

*Clackamas Literary Review*: "Brothers," "The Shovel Speaks"

*Crazyhorse*: "Horse," "On those Mountains Night Is Falling"

*Folio*: "Horse Latitudes"

*Gulf Coast*: "Door" (p. 7), published as "Front Matter"; "Marsh Hawk on the Paddock Bridge"

*Green Mountains Review*: "Tongue," "Strike"

*Hayden's Ferry Review*: "The Kite, the Wires"

*HUBBUB*: "Too Easy Questions on Lonely Roads," "Key"

*Notre Dame Review*: "Ampersand in Mind," "Above the River," "The Lock's Anatomy"

*NEO* (Portugal): "Vespertide," "Aforementioned Gate," "Shook Foil," "Landfall"

*Packingtown Review*: "Doves"

*Passages North*: "Relic Tour"

*Phoebe*: "Luster"

*Poetry Kanto* (Japan): "Horses Seen from the Plane," "Sky Harbor" (p. 63), published as "Sun Corridor"

*ReDivider*: "Tinderbox"

*Seneca Review*: "Bird in a Box," published as "Aleph in Hand"

*The Platt Valley Review*: "Sky Harbor" (p. 3)

*Third Coast*: "Infertility"

*9th Letter*: "Manmade Seas"

Some of these poems appear in chapbooks *Portents Aside*, published by Two Dogs Press; and *Horses Seen from the Plane*, Pudding House Chapbook Series.

The author wishes to express gratitude for an individual artist's grant from The Arizona Commission on the Arts, which was awarded during the composition of this manuscript; The Writer's Workshop of The University of Nebraska at Omaha for institutional support; and The University Office of Sponsored Programs & Research.

Many thanks to: Chris Dombrowski, Megan Gannon, James Jay, Joanna Klink, Chris Porter, Natalie Peeterse, Lisa Sandlin, and Joshua Ware.

FOR M & M

# CONTENTS

Oh valley without mother height, where everything sleeps
a horrible halftone, without refreshing rivers, without beginnings of love.
Oh voices and cities that pass galloping on a finger
pointed at bald unity.

—César Vallejo



A key will be my dwelling,
The feint of a fire the heart confirms;
And the air whose talon held it.

—René Char

1

# SKY HARBOR

Our nettled craft of exits,
    metal's sheen lost
in fading southern ranges, our devotion
    to iron filings drawn from the dirt, jets
tilt in sunlight.
    Travelers, acolytes caned en masse
amid the false shimmer of origin, of mirror,
    wince at the quivering patter
of circles widening on dusty parcels and cinder blocks,
    and there's a faint guttering at the end of roads,
a flare on the other side.  How else to bring what won't
    come to us on its own
a bit closer?
    An approximation's fist in the skull, heat, a pulse
is drawn out into vacant shoeshine grottoes,
    into the mouths of engines, but promise
of such ungregarious surprises
    brought us here together
where the sun pulls like a razor in the nurse's hand—
    don't look at it—
fire-lit, concussive, suggestive of the pivot and fall
    of the great foot.
So ripples splay
    as drinking lips
break the surface,
    kilter igniting then dampening,
an eye behind a lid,
    a toy eight ball's future.
And snared and capering on a wire,

there's a yellow party balloon,
smiley face on both sides, head
   turning *not-me-not-me-not-*
until an engine's wake snaps it gone.
   Is the desert, sweet tourniquet and wound beneath
our metal shell, also an echo?  How the drowning
   must forget
what they dive after.
   As with deep water, the desert is
for the forgetful, for the prize—for those who
   lose their grip.
Those we dive after.  Two sparrows
   are trapped in the crowded terminal—a little girl
looks up.

# STRIKE

So close, the sky
stopped as the clouds
cleared, as if through a keyhole
in the rock I caught a glimpse
of fire, uninhabitable with nothing to feed it,
or was it sunlight on lake water?
How to surface and know
that the lightning
was not for us, that the strike
was not ours? Still echoing in
our ribs there uttered
what had waited a lifetime to
move through us and be heard.  Its storm cell
halved the valley, its violence at
a distance—a towel slipping from your
waist by lamplight—
was gone.  Erased then
restored, unblemished in
draws and hoof prints, standing
water eclipsed by
wing beats in scattered
ozone, as if thunder had
cracked the sky's underbelly
of sleeping scavengers, falling birds
turning noonday into milky iridescence
half darkening the desert scrub.
Still bearing leaves, the tree
that took the strike
gave it to the bull now dead

on its side.  Your hands
spanned valleys to
reach me, where unflinching
in the animal's eye, the horizon held
neither of us.  Which role was ours,
now that to draw closer would
pull us to its center, would break
the circuits of courting birds,
the dampening void of
thermals, then wave after wave
of vultures descending, the pact
between us sinuous, still
warm to first touch, to what
had stopped stirring beneath
the surface, your voice
taut, its twinning
undone only to tangle and
bunch before the mottled flanks
that were swaying at their tugs?  Devouring
yet devoured, at what point
did we vanish, where nothing
would be lost, where of two worlds
known to us—one being *danger*,
the other, *domain*—
neither would have us.

# DOOR

In one version of our lives together
we never leave the shore.

The barman, all too happy to drop ice into our tumblers
and close the door behind him, lets us stay
inside the solarium facing the canal

and rain, a tonsure of gray skin,
ouzo clouding drops upon panes never reaching
the pebble floor.  Our room could be taken
to higher ground.
                    Water, as when dreaming
of something written, holds us.  To look away—
would it leave us where an eye had been?

Once, on another shore, we came upon a dead owl,
tiny sockets emptied and filled, an alveolar world
of bones composing what is not water, what we see
as spaces opening, say as doors
whose voices the stranded tend to hear, whom we address

though we feign talking to the ever reaching.
Though we feign talking to each other.

# INFERTILITY

Your glass not finished breaking.  But it's my alarm sounding.  Who carries whom into our valley of little motels?  *The wind and rock joining hands to catch us, a salty squall torrefies.*  Your word, *torrefy*.  You can have that because I like to hear you read it to me.  My odd rain on parking lots.  Your mottled hawk adrift.  Nobody's multiplex.  Your corona in the sooty wake, your trucks, but my green corrugation.  Our gleam in a light.  As for studio thunder:  your sheet of aluminum shaken, but we're both in yellow slickers.  Your boots.  My spigot.  Stop laughing.  Your bird in a box, but I'll be the first to say I stole it.  If I've been carrying what I'm looking for into the heart of your aggravation, that's not my fault.  That hand-written note from your mother saying *I'm so proud of you.*  That's yours.  My roach in a window screen.  But take it.  We came upon the amnesia of the washed-out festival at the same time.  Coincidence.  Kismet.  Keep the crags, but they were mine.  As for strong horses.  Strong horses could be anyone's.  But when strong horses' limbs are lain to rest, those horses belong to Lucretius.  So if the horses are dreaming.  Let me finish please.  The dreams of strong horses.  The horses' dreams are free.

# HORSE

Among sixteen horses on the western slope
    weathering sleet and sunshine, reflecting field-lit
contours, there is a first horse, one where I might
    bring my face to its cheek, feel the eyelash of its thought,
see myself reflected there, hand extended—how it had seen
    an early flash upon a winter clarity restaged on the iris
of its companion, and they whitened together in the comet's return.
    They bolted at the man of Tarsus kept blind, who kept his name
staggering among the husks, the sleepers beneath
    patches of ice and tufts of bunchgrass.  This horse watched
my mother as a girl passing in a train, fence posts
    pulling to where the two-lane county road brought me
to the length of the animal's moment, which is always, skin
    taut around the mouth, older than the skies that cured the hide-locked
region around its eye—avuncular, and at center
    an eddy of weather and dust that sifted the afternoons and roads,
the cave aperture where the stone held its ground.
    The animal did not move.  I came no closer.

# DOOR

We know ourselves as two doors,
        fathers seeing the first from far away,
mothers coming en masse to the second.
        Both hear the key's indelible
scrawl revise itself in the second-thought
        of oil, of tumblers, the lock willing
its bolt through selvedge
        and again back, the generations
crossing the foyer in nightdress,
        backlit motes adrift on stale air
out of the current's reach. The sun
        is going down, the sun is on
the other side of the world. Fathers
        crowd the narrows homeward,
changing their lives, telling
        themselves for the last time, footsteps
scattering birds from the trees, they are
        jarred by the lock's trapdoor striker,
ungiving at the legion of useless keys.
        At odd hours mothers wake to all the
words they know will pass through us,
        our candle-lit byways,
light-piqued fissure of escutcheon
        blown out. Fathers then mothers before the frame,
broken then mended to hold us, where at one
        they whisper please, at the second
they kick it through.

# FATHERS

In the terraced room whose floors are stairs

                      between two

doors room enough for them the fathers have

                      come for us as if

attracted by our talk of them how they

                      shielded us

from what we are unprepared to see shield us

                      more they want to

endanger us take us along before headlights

                      mountain roads

where more pictures will be taken take us

                      to the man who

looks to be sleeping merely posing as what

                      they wait in

the poorly-lit-in-between dressed for pictures

                      children keep they are

confused trying to keep what they kept

                      together and left

leave us they have come to fail a little more to

                      wait for us to come

home to interrogate the time to rend the hour

                      from us they know

we cannot sleep as if toward a coughing child

                      they step inside with

water without knocking through thin walls many

                      rooms they hear us

# TONGUE

Small the capsules split, this sleight of wing

                                the swallow tucks into its nook among

the tiles, small the seed's migration, viaticum

                                afloat, scattered in the courtyard's heft, whose

sky is made more distant, staved clouds swift, and

                                small the undulating scene that the sun

leaves, the mallows' stalks back-lit, afternoon

                                tinctured through grillwork and offertory

door once heaped with still life—pocked

                                fruit, the rabbit's skinned likeness, left there—what

turned within the walls toward the waiting

                                hands of penitents is gone, the refectory tables,

luminous currents of seeds through rooms,

                                vestibular as if our lives were passage, our

silence a bulwark against the narrows, these

                                packed enactments, motes that umber ornamental

groves and the well head sealed with a stone,

                                carillons long taken for war's metal, the tower

gaping, the reminder latent, small this kneeling

                                place, as or as if by the sea, smaller still

the life whose breath reaches into cold air, into a

                                fragile bowl and not the world that filled it, our

blood a knell, what voices the welter brings, this

                                husk, the insect flown.

# BIRD IN A BOX

From the corner of your eye
to a shoebox at the foot of night's stair,
          from when you held it—still
     warm between the cupped palms of
your hands—to heat
          leaving the blood—*like that*,
from not a child to lift
          its lid, to someone's first death
all the time, as feathers flip back
               and forth on its collision mark, from one
     anticipated clearing to another,
from azoth torn from the hour, breast-
                    down with its back
to me, and for me to follow,
               to the selfsame current
     that bore it from *always*
to *now*—windfall of loosestrife,
                    the bird funneled into a double-
          paned window, current toying the tufts of
under-down from the smallest hearts
     of larger hearts, as one might
                    turn it over, yet always with its back to me—
          from the arc of its name, call it
     a stray, a spool of thread through
               thicket, of searing line,
     to indigo fluting through tears, from
the glyph's load that is too much,
                    to a hand that a larger hand

may—if it stops shaking—
    close around, distance no more
        than a crescent in the sky and the wish
    to replace *distance*
with *proximity*, and then take it.

# HORSES SEEN FROM THE PLANE

Ticking with melting ice,
trestles buoy themselves in wisps across the river.

The rusting frame, a bridge,
a derelict carnival ride

sinks into the sticks.  More weather is coming,
and the way home, another flight

of the alone to the alone, telescopes out
into a block of slick Tarmac,

where piled like euthanized pandas in an open cart
our bags await their throwers.

Through the metallic winks
of the climb-out, the once manifold

shards, the cracked surfaces
are, at a glimpse, whole again

in the sinew and luster
of distant horses the wind is braiding

at full gate, the farthest
reach of lightning, irretrievable and

funneling up the draw
through a fissure

of sunlight
you are just beginning to see.

# AMPERSAND IN MIND

To see through the portion of a body that is
                               nobody, to stave off the pitch and yaw
               of advancing forms, strides

echo what will never be
                       seen through—
                                      what anticipates your step,
thistles taller than corn or mother
                       of your own grace-noted
       stutter-step,
               flushed and unwanted
                       cutlery between boot-falls,

as bats wheel after
                       the tick of moths
       drawn toward your lantern,
                       whose coil is chiming inside the glass,
tangled ring in light's hollow, with no one

               to catch you
               listening—for footsteps, wingbeats—
                                              much less if you fall
into their clusters of stalks crowding the trail, or

are they drinkers at a wake,
               who, at changing the subject,

fall silent and wait for you to pass,

                        for nightfall to clot

the lantern's reach,

    the onset unctuous,

                            as if the gas were left on

        and thought's wick guttered there

    in each fiber, each barb, fine hairs more needle

    than hair,

        call it fire, harboring fugitive birds

                    caught inside an inky frame

and from what spills, the way back tapers into

                a dimly lit trickle, into watershed,

the periphery stirring on all sides

      reaching in, the vial is on its side,

          the cardinal points

                joining hands, cracking black.

# PORTENTS ASIDE

Of those who've seen its tree,
            of those saying "cradled," who prefers
    "caught," and who thought at first windblown
sack or flag shadow so close
            to the school, and of those praying this weather
              might, by way of
high pressure or dust, spare

            our children, who looks to their cruelty,
    though the crotch of the tree is
            too high for them, and so having
had its tree at your back,
            for whom did it rise again, and if
    it did rise again—say, while driving
away only to have
            it there in the windshield—who
                    turned around to keep it
behind them?

            Of those preferring "crux," who sees
a natural order, and who finds it easier to
              push it aside and keep driving, and
who expected something much
        worse—some event more
spectacular to make the town feel so
        small, and since they are
plentiful—"common" the guide tells us—who
            has ever found one like it, and who cared
    for them alive, or

marveled at their design until now, and

                            who blames the boy, or the stone,

          and of those blaming the boy, who calls it sister,

                and who blames the absence

                    of a father who hunts, and of those who

        exonerate the boy, who points to the presence of a father

           who doesn't hunt who, like the mother,

must defend the boy, and

        who blames the air, and of those


secretly praising the aim, who

        hopes to polish the skull as a keepsake for such a trifle

that towns worry over—

                    bauble that our talk moves through even

now it could be in some keeper's hand, so

        among the sayers

          of crotch or crux, who will climb the tree?

Who waits for it to fall?

# DOVES

All our fitful nights are cast upon the motel wall,
everyone in their frame, the lens' vantage peering down
upon us:  honeycombs of near-sleep, knee to chest,

like flies twitching in a carapace.  If you squint, you can
trace each sleeper's eyes struggling beneath thin surfaces,
a rubber curtain the nurse throws in a well-lit ward,

tonight half our lives are lit up in the tenement
rows recidivists share, each worry deeper the mattress.
Who didn't want to dig through the earth, the sun gone down

with no one to call us in.  Each shovelful brings us
seconds closer to falling through a stranger's daylight.

Mangled hand pressed against the dusk, hand missing fingers.
The latitudes come quickly with the scarecrow in my
rearview mirror, arrivals as faithful as chain-link

that keeps us from sleeping under an overpass.
If I keep driving like this, towns and county lines snap
beneath the tires, seams in the pavement or dormant rows

in the fields, the fields behind me like wind-pulled sheets from
the line, flags from poles, downed power lines.  Scarecrow, you are
as steadfast as the interstate's roughened margin that

wakes us from drifting, that keeps us awake at the wheel,
dear proxy whose pace matches my own, keep me from sleep.

Doves are growing and the boots of the father who shoots
and cleans them wither away as the half-forgotten
fear reverses itself in the doves' eyes, at once holes

in pocked stone where a lost species might hide, and a lens
through which we measure how far they are behind us,
how we keep this pace ahead of those for whom sands sift

away, even one as close to the ground as the boy
with doves at his feet, viscous droplets of something sweet
an arm had ladled onto each body's bedding and

made a dove's eye.  His reflection floats as floodwaters
hold an aftermath's sky, and the waters are rising.

What we breathe is broken.  If we don't take care, bathing
in the buzzing ambergris of the weekly motel
as the wee hours' smallest part's flicker ignites, childhood's

last skewered poppy soaked in gasoline passes before us
and we will breathe, inhalation that is laughter or
the first loose footholds of one who has farther to fall

and never hits the ground.  Motes of warm rust, feathers, salt
not from the sea fill the hollow scarab nature that
hinged its wing.  Falling is the heart of metals that brought

doves to us.  On the corrugated roof the weathers
tick, and morning's gunmetal whistles beneath the door.

Vast the downy province of the bird on its side whose
brushstrokes tessellate and ring its eye whose papery
lid is pulled over a false gem's iridescence.

As far as you can see, squatters' fires punctuate the field.
How to flee the clink of newly minted metal plates
beneath the veterans' skin, the mandibles of a

mother chewing, the tearing tissue paper cough of
the baby in the reeds, the click and coo of he who
assures me that I can, if I want, any time now

stop screaming.  Spilling from dispatch is my name, and my
hands are behind my back.  Stay put don't make us chase you.

Consider the skulls of doves weighing nothing in your hands,
their echo's weight cannot keep them on the palm's surface,
hatchlings whose tongues have fallen from their heads at birth.

The hunter's skin is your skin and it scurries with the
shadows of frightened birds as you move from dove to dove,
tufts of feathers and blood at your feet, you will find

a stainless steel bowl of viscera.  Footprints fill with seeds,
unearthed and brittle, and what ground will have them?
From meager heights doves are falling, the syllables, their

songs trace the arc of their fall.  Like the labored breaths of
he who climbs a chair, all too scared to stay there, steps back down.

But when I am allowed to hold the dove's heart, wet edge
at the center of my fist, just after the punch is thrown,
at the moment my hand opens, like a cured wound

it will, without the weight of its fool body, rise through
branches and poles, whose flags and wires as with wires in a
window that the school desk won't break through.  Unlike scarcity

or fear spanning the desolate draws between the seen
and the departed, doves are buoyant with rain or loam.
Fools will tie a string to it, will ask for more hearts from

the metal bowl.  This open hand—like counting
off my reasons—I cannot stop watching it rise.

# THE KITE, THE WIRES

How far can you walk away and still see the boy on the pole
rising above your neighborhood,

                                   at your stepping behind an
outermost grove then back-peddling

       porch steps, hiding
behind your mother reading, looking over her

shoulder, wondering
if his face—growing smaller in the window—will change as you
pull away—

       this bullied boy whose mouth you make out moving in
what?—in pain?  in awe?  Can he look into your house

and still see you not sleeping,

                            you who put him there, drawing away
as from all accidental fires,

              for he is not the one who is lonely,
nor has he forgotten the ruse you used
to coax him into

the wires after the silk tail which is swaying in bedtime air,

nor is he trying to get down—as if he wanted to keep company
the dragon he had climbed into electricity to save,

                 which belongs to live wires, to your seeing
how far you can retreat and never lose him, never run out of
       what you would not do to take him down,

                     yet you open

more distance, more straining eyesight to catch a glimpse where?  Lost
dinnertime sky's lavender still holds him in your sight, where he

waits no longer stranded for you
                                    to pull this morning's curtain and
to still want him there.

# BROTHERS

Who among brothers spoke of the deathbed bequeathal
stars become—one by one

Xmas lights on the eves of no one home?
There is a part of me that will never speak.

Trees go on pouring themselves
backhanded into the night, a wash of sky

limns their reach, our limbs
spill onto the patio, voices harrowed about

how good
television used to be—O those

unforgettable nights in front of the TV.
The same caught kite in the window,

in the weathers, age arrives in each other,
but we, the legendary trespassers

have surfaced empty
handed late in life to catch our breath

at the verdant edge of our mother's lawn.
Like love, the process leaves me

shapeless, easily mistaken for you,
perpetually on the brink of leaving home.

Help me to the cup's edge, to the station—
let's leave together.

This one's on me—had we
a cocktail car, had we a train.

# VESPERTIDE

As if we could pass through
the first star's slow pulse, star edge
hewn above a line of poplars,
the ornamental ash, the gravel drive
tapering away to dry leaves as
the moment closes and the lamp's dregs
scour the room for flaws,
for cracks of emergence, a spider's
familiar aperture, which is now
and now's attendant capture
in cerements twitching
concentrically in the hunter's
tumbling weave.  How long ago
our mother wrapped us
in a towel at our reluctant rise
from warm water, a brother
then one brother more, my turn
to enter the chill air, no more five
more minutes—now,
the minutes' gloss catching
the spider's flawless mark, which
shatters the seconds, which are
too many to hold—let go,
the sky a lock's lamina, whose latch
releases at the tumblers' final turn
behind the tree line, which
for all its mirroring
dampens, as with a heavy keepsake

dropped, or the glint of a
swimmer's chest, my hands
sinking out of reach
into water deep enough to slip away
and be taken.

# RELIC TOUR

A pillowslip
tumbles down the barrel of an alley.

The moon's progress when clouds are swift
hints that perhaps the world is

faster than once thought.
Perhaps the mind is nothing more than this town

your dog is lost in or a daughter
sight-reading music from an heirloom hymnal—

call out and each awkward measure
of the songbook grafts your voice with hers

and is lost in the blustering narrows between
buildings.  How not to imagine her

book's engravings of
bubbles blown from the mouths of youths,

lutes played in the swirls
of the many drowned?

To hear—*by day  the shad-ows  slip  a-way At eve-ning  back they creep…*
is to think of a flickering

window in a widow's walk—
of a house too far to be heard.

Like the cry of a gull when landlocked,
look up and find the same cat treed or

find a weather vane or hear a woman's voice
say your first name

then your last for the first time
in a long time.  A bell rings

from the courthouse square.
Tonight the same pair of shoes

dangles from the wire, left
then right finding each other.

Maybe no one is falling at this hour.
The town is a toy breed

and the toy breed is named after a mineral
mined here.  In the once bordello

now bar where a gunslinger's head
could be removed and you could

drink bourbon from the killer's ceramic body
a painter painted a small black dog

front paws on the inner thigh
of a girl who worked the rooms upstairs,

her face gauzed in throes of weather you want
never to carry away anyone.

One foot off the velvet divan
fills a boot sizes too big.  No one remembers

why we mined the mineral
or what the mineral was for.

Who allows the guide to light a match
to turn his helmet off
to blow the last wick out, might see

what is left of a spent mine,
what generations
of horses see, what a man sees

long after he is lowered by a rope
at the waist into a kiln—a mine within
a mine—weighed down, hands

clutching a sledge
and told from the surface to swing
at manganese caked on its walls.

In the phosphoric dregs of
the guide's match
the eyes are slowly broken

the bad news.  Off light's tether
retracing steps not
offered, adrift in currents

the kiln
becomes your study,
the man's motion, his carbide lamp

cutting out, glimpses flicker in the kiln's mouth
as walls fall away in sheets
at each pass, a bell's tongue

flailing to remember
its hymn, what he breathes, what he
says to himself beneath the clouds,

the wires, at whose mercy—closing your eyes
does not come close—the guide promises
before his match is out.

# WHEN THE SHOVEL SPEAKS

The children's ambition
is to vanish into their hole-to-be,
to leave home, to journey through,
but can they deepen it, live
inside it, travel on the shovel's back
past fiber optics and
sewer lines to gather
doubloons, potsherds the gas
company overlooked, until
one of them spies daylight
through a fissure, noontime
from the other side of
the world beneath this vacant lot?
But caliche,
hardpan, duricrust, mixed
carbonates inches beneath us, the shallows
upon which drifts a once pavilion of bone—
human and rodent, maxillae
cornices, plague
bearers whose cycles of mandibles
wane, dormant plague, root
matter, the skeletal drifts
through whose past, through
whose destiny we travel
the inches and go
no further... and had the children
but a stone to pry loose, a circle to
widen a bit farther to find
an edge to it, as sleepwalkers

look for a threshold
in the dream and never find the door.
O father of grave mounds, caliche, keeper
of wine above ground, bone-like
basin soil and bones
stir upon, who goes deeper,
you decide.

# ABOVE THE RIVER

Steep grade,
            prismatic noon
splitting blue, wind and sunlight
        shot through the throats
of birds.  We were thirsty,
            ankles bent in durable tufts
and dust of a far and arid bank,
        the only way up and out,
scrambling loose basalt,
            bloody-kneed toward their
wheels.  And if water
        had been in our canteens,
would we have seen them
            like this, or the water?
—mercurial, or better yet a wire
        cutting in half a veiny heart,
folding itself away,
            boring through granite
—the great canopy
        above us so weather-eaten
and painful to see, I
            looked away to write down
the words *ether-torn*,
        but misread as either torn
apart or mended, birds
            being both, calling out a name,
uttering *season, sunlight, river,*
        knowing.  As if we heard

a warning—no, we
        brought warning with us.
Shadows pocked the slope beneath
        a kaleidoscopic helix of crows.

# SHOOK FOIL

A far reflection without a source
       as inside an old camera whose curtain falls, each face
in the crowd searched the others—your face
       was among them in the clouded
mirror, which for once looked closer.  Every eye
       was with me.  The crowd was tired, up all night, as if
they had left a roadside vigil or an execution
       to walk the cul-de-sacs and canals,
the air-born dregs catching—who could say what—a swath
       of hue draped—someone said the words *black light*,
but that wasn't right.  Behind abandoned staging areas
       and empty towers, a pulse, and beyond that
we hoped for fields, and beyond the storied razors
       joining hands, fences where decisions have been made for us,
there was a half-prayed-for breach in this belated age
       where a tree and light were not fire.
A cypress, our fingers clinging to the idea like insect shells,
       noon split where moths' short lives were
hidden again somewhere in the carpet of mouths
       that we've convinced ourselves secretly longs
for the inevitable.  Between safe houses the minutes
       frighten us, and the gate shuts us out from what can
hold light or cast shadow or be eaten—
       gates rendering the days crawl spaces—whispers
of an angel's loosening whir.

Shard from a gathering underbelly that once shielded us,
old weather caught as if lightless fire and
    chemical damp had risen to catch form, between
silver and glass, the gloss of cherished numbers
    taken from us, I searched the frontage roads for you
and dreamt of what might burn.

# TINDERBOX

Afternoon ashes
its dread from both ends.
Not a drop, but resin
beading from gasping
heartwood.  A fountain
in the center of the town
about to burn evaporates
as it pulses.  Wilting in the over-
flow of what little remains,
we while away
the unwelcome thrum
of zephyrs in the wires,
thunder or smoke, take
your pick.  And turn it off.
And turn off the dream.
And the sea that we all dream
where your hair is dark
from stepping out of the rain.
Between waking's slow
inroad to the interior,
and night's ethered rag,
sleep digs a hole
into a dawn emptied
of yips and calls.  The pilot
makes a precarious pass,
a shadow between buildings,
leaves warping the water
plane's props.

Exile is coming for us and
prompts a weary nod
from the unnerved
volunteers on the truck,
the hills they drive into
water-logged, beached.
Dusk's tired residue of
*who-are-you-behind-the-curtain?*
Streetlights at noon.
No curtain but fire striding
through the psaltery thicket
of pines that once veiled
the yellowing draw,
its slope blackened,
and through our celluloid
frame, or as a finger
pressed upon us in the dark
movie theater,
its fingerprint behind
our eyelids, upon our eyes—
that can't be the sun
falling through the haze then
vanishing, the horizon
smudged with thunderheads,
and there, with its back
to us, rain wandering off
in a paper gown.

# TOO EASY QUESTIONS ON LONELY ROADS

A turbine,
a conduit-tangled hive
glassed-in, so that a motorist
—if there were one
at this hour, on this hill—
might see what's at stake
in keeping the hospital's
power plant humming,
the road curves from here
then drops, asphalt
evanescing into streaks
of halogen, moonlight
from the trauma center's
landing lights, a windsock
mirrored against the
oncology building, a kink
in our descent through
a burgeoning fortress of
services, toward
the metal works below
cutting scrap late into the night
behind a snarl of bindweed
and chain-link, a rusted
fence between watcher and
welder's arc, cleaving
minimus of fire peered at
through leaves flaring out to
watermark a blinking—
now blinded eye—

and what white knuckling thought
won't let go it holds
against its chest,
as if *my god* were the words
the branding residue of magnesium
says when the heroic mind
cannot.

# HEARTLAND INDEX

As for the hemlock

As with wood, beleaguered by hinges

Becalmed before the chapel glass

Bulb burned out behind the glass

Countersunk as tumblers tossed to allow a bolt

Escutcheon—all there is to see, takes its key, so

If there is insect song, look for a mechanism

Moonrise, what eyes you from the back of its head, has many eyes

One can harvest more than teeth

Sunlight tinkers the corrugation of the praise center

The center whose field is a carpet of mouths

The field waxes proverbial

The nidus where light is laid

The pawl finds its wheel, the groove finds its bolt

The selvage takes its bolt

Their carousel needed for its wood

Their warehouse on fire

They are horses, horses stay the mark, steadfast, fixed on what's to come

Those without are laved in veins of a damp inferior grade

To sinew the trapdoor striker

Verily as dry goods kicked out from under the felon

What funnels overhead is unmanned

What geigers in its pot is not an egg

When the lock is perennial, nothing is ajar

You heard the silo spill its memory of bats

You heard the bees—nothing grows, there are no bees

# MANMADE SEAS

The earth is lying to us
again, its promise that the past,
its aggregate of gnats
would, if we stop digging
into the silt for signs,
stay put—that behind us,
the faraway stone
that once held its light
and caught our eye
would rekindle on the horizon.
Who heard them chanting us
deeper into winter, into drought,
or was it summer that passed
for sunlight on the alley of little
motels, what pried
open the inversion's pall?
From the sheen of tailings,
there spilled onto the corrugation and ample
pavement a mist that
no one could call rain.
What a curse
yields when reaching back
into disputed roots,
is a surprise, a trickle of
water running over stones,
whose exile or refuge
will never be enough.  If furthest
bears us here,
furthest appears again

at a paved edge,
an airstrip beacon panning
a low ceiling,
calling home an engine
echo in the veil,
which is more an outboard
whine, an engineer
to plumb the channel, or more
volunteers to dredge
the shallows for the vanished, a swimmer's
wish beneath the
thrum of tension wires,
is our wish to lower
ourselves down the steep
shore, to push
out into the current—that it
never bears us
to an old wished-for source,
an island exposed,
whose story and burial clays
are not lost
beneath the floodlit surface,
does not seem to
matter.  The search must
end for the day
at the sweeping hands of anchorpersons,
where dry docks
reach out until the mesa
ends in nightfall,

an extension cord and rope
ladder for a squatter
inside the hull, his stove's
flue cut through
the cabin, taking what will
burn.  Who heard
the news?  *That was*
*Thursday*, the voice inside
the cabin tells us.
*Tuesday he drowned.*

# MARSH HAWK ON THE PADDOCK BRIDGE

Over seamless fields, drainages
to deeper water, the eye and re-firing neural paths
are dove-rapt and hunting with feeding birds.

Rictal breath visible in the cold,
primary coverts splay and mantle the dove
peppered in blood, liturgical as a curtain

now offered up on memory's rusted girder.
Tendons shimmer, fibrous and oblong gore.
Trace back the dove

leaving the safety of the maple's lattice,
accruing context through cortex
to slide its shadow across the snowy field.

As from a wellspring, from hippocampus through
limbic byways, relive the dove plucked on the wing.
There are the rough-edged holes

where blood melts through the snow
and leads to fallen aftermath, the hollowed-out reliquary,
as synapses make my tangled way,

where a dove is obliterated, restaged, rived
and steaming on the bridge.
Blood's metallic warmth, like rust

courses through the Papez Circuit, and I'm
cleaning game birds again, or my grandfather
is in his wheelchair, staring at his hands

in disbelief.  As if they don't belong to him.
From hippocampus through cortex,
from the maple, wing shadow glides out,

and back to hippocampus,
back to the disk-shaped face of the hawk.
Where within its eye-ring

the parabola sharpens, the circuit hollows
the cell that memory becomes, fovea from which
the heart, and not the eye, might see.

Retrace *capturing* and *caught*, re-travel synapses:
my head is on my mother's chest, her heart
beating through her blouse; my body draped

against my father, sweat and bourbon, fried chop
and vinegar on his shirt, he's singing *Deep
in the Heart of Texas*.  Remember, and again

the news breaks, our child won't come to term,
blood before the ultrasound, the fields and copses
that the dove sees while in the hawk's grip,

the doctor wants me to sit down, the bird
falls from its branch, and every stone I ever throw
is falling back to me.

# KEY

Consider from the door
what you want protected,     a country where
the bolt holds its ground          and          wood gives way
to be patched along the lintel,     threshold
          where lifetimes are sifted on either side
and blow away.     Where are they?
*Just a door ajar that oceans are*—you read,
yet the lock works          in terms of one
and many,          bits of broken glass in their wake,
an auger's tongue speaking the faces
in wood grain                    —*It's me, open the door.*
Pollen in the groves dispatched in moonlight,
stencil dabs of bats          and whip-poor-wills
when you think it safe          to open the door—
see earth auger.                    On either side, there are
the last-ditch efforts in the inclement that you,
that your children become,     beneath a wheel
that's never oiled,                    a screamer on the bridge—
the keyhole          and its ticking lock.  Are you
bound to re-lose what you've lost?     As if the key
*may at pleasure join that which nature hath severed,*
burnished catalyst,     second thinker,     more than teeth.
What couples tenderly is me,   fibs the key.
You can tell from the scarred sill,          this house is not
as old as you thought          and on either side, you
know each other well.

# AFOREMENTIONED GATE

*Haven*, I wanted
you to say then found
the seat beside me empty.  How long

had I been alone, how far back
were the abandoned cars, their engines
running, the other drivers

climbing with me, each at a distance,
the steep shoulder into the trees?
The longed-for roads were harder to

retrace when I looked away.
We had driven in silence,
our road a cut in the rind, the plateau

not yet crested, one switchback in a chain,
serrations of scrub then pines.  At an edge
the thread of cars waited for wreckage

to be cleared up ahead,
and past the mile marker and white cross,
a makeshift cenotaph, where a survivor had written *my*

*hero* in gold.  In what time we had
we were caught
tracing *hermit tracks*, we called them,

trails fading into the brush, a wire
fence, its padlock—*a tongue,*
*but never heart*, you said, *left on the latch to rust.*

The way from there
sharpened into a far point above metals idling in the hills.
It had been nothing to pull

the barbed wire over my head
to drop down the far saddle into
such scarcity, into shattered

mirrors, the shale
let go of the sky at dusk—like skin
the deciduous veins of a valley arrived,

tree bark reflecting an evening emptied of
moonlight.  New leaves
rattled in the calm.  I wasn't far

into the lichen straights, yet at which
moment's apogee was the repertoire
of fear only beginning

to spend itself—*haven*, I heard
myself saying—*have I ever lived here,*
*have I no other choice?*

# LUSTER

divides—pairs off, falls away like coin
and shadow in the wind—
                               framed by a hand
not stayed, with tallow—smoke
            threading through thatch,

*manger's tear* as if we spoke of leaf-shape or
a plant's common name that we suddenly remember,
                 yet animal fat sears on stone,


                               popping,
and late afternoon thickens, a yellow dye on your arms
and thighs, not snowmelt's metal and oil,
but pollen
            choking crags in rock and beetle-kill,

scaly juniper bark, a din hushed.  Then a scrape of a knife
                 pulls you away from me.


Consolation is too thin, hands, my hands,
one on each side of the door
                 as it shuts, *may the living*
*please you again*, says the change

in the weather, snow a wish to wake
again to gossamer, their makers
                               aloft somewhere, seed cotton, vines

whispering *innuendum* whose root is splitting granite and is *nuere,*
and what was promised us,
—as if anything is ever promised—

whir and shard, cold's damp underbelly—will never be granted.
Straw-like tittering falling from eaves,

to nod—*nūmen*, holy hint, where one nod
in two words, to hope, have gone to work on me—

is to cut away the margins where I might
hold you by the shoulders
and bear this, grief's shadow newly minted across your face,
and mine, currency of this

as bats spill from our rotted soffits,
numbers' swift patchwork, a weather's
practice, loss which keeps seeing us to a far point of memory,

horizon ever at a blind gallop toward us,
a desert we can no longer cross,
of considerable—I can't call it darkness—
where upon—in you—
far objects appear.

# LANDFALL

Beneath eyelids the desert
reaches into every corner, into
the numbed extremities
of the port whose gulls' and swifts' lilt
vanishes before the village—a child's
laughter carried by water.
No longer beneath the surface, water pleats
where a last animal struggles.
Dawn's face turns toward us
another bout of
warming metal, enough to touch, to see
further what such skies
sear, what is not men, what is not rigging,
sudden cliffs
and hills, the drugged sleep
of a burn victim that is my sleep.
And how the hull, unburdened of
necessities, adrift in the doldrums, is witness
to this slow wake of convulsing water,
and the cliffs' jury of scowls too
dimly lit, mistaken shoulders
down to the edge, to the bell's
matins, down to what still prospect in
the chapel hold, to the tower's
portion before us
of opalescence
against bleaching opalescence.

# ON THOSE MOUNTAINS NIGHT IS FALLING

Behind them
Are faces we demand blessings of,
Ports we will be missing
En route to, a cluster of trees where it's hard
Not to linger in the sounds of our
Names calling us in from a doorway
Without a door.  I will carry the cold of this place
Where neither caller nor called is known
Yet to look at anything for a long time,
The ridgeline, a listener in the eye
As one corrugated rooftop among the shantytown
Catches dusk then gilds in a murky
Keysmith's window, is to know
Something of the unlivable heavens
A lifetime becomes.
High in the deadwood hour
Where no bird should be
The woodcock's eye reaches back to steps
Taken here, footprints sinking into alluvia
Long after its river leaves the map.  A bird
In the periphery whose call is clamor, is pure
As a cul-de-sac of rainwater
In a neighborhood of empty houses,
Where at one I lay hands flat.  The grain
Is warm.  Is there a fire behind it?  My son
Is breathing there with all that I have told him,
All that narrowly survives is in his hand,
Exposed from the bedding now closing.
Sweet cargo of *once-when-I.*

# HORSE LATITUDES

If the desert is the recto and my lifetime watching it the verso

am I half desert, half daylight through
                              keyhole, half door, half word—am I
half of Monday's shimmering key, and in adding this impossible sum

cursed, fashioned
            to go no deeper into its salt and pith?

To squint into the plaits, into the clotting swells,
                              eyes fancy themselves wings, weavers
that weft and warp through
                  the draws, through weeks.  They carry

these human days no more than wing
                              or womb, all that keeps one world from another,

nuptial rings we pass into Monday, going as far as sand

strewn with murmurs back
                  to me:  murmur before the door.
Door that does not open, door that wills
                              a bit more rumor from these
lips, just a little more daylight
                  through a lock's narrow way.

# SKY HARBOR

Soot falls onto the foothills,
onto the nimbus of Phoenix in the haze,
its worn-toothed horizon

of grabens and rooftops beleaguered with
little past, and its present
little more than

a thief's hour, which has caught
me dozing by the unblemished murk
of the reservoir,

where stepping from shadows
is my dead father
muttering into a jacklight's wick

that will not light,
his shirt and furrowed brow
a brambly thatch that waters

assembled seasons ago, his body
giving way as
country music fades to talk radio

from his pickup
—*my pickup*
parked by the water's edge.

The way here, the once uncrowned
and headlit turns
taken late at night through

foothills, is a wide and straight
grid of outskirts
that drops the eye down what's left

of a river against the dam.
My hands pull the weighted line
and gizzard bait from

the surface, and the radio's
panel of experts tells me what the next offensive
means.  The tugging

fish, barbed and
jaundiced channel cat, has no use
for daylight, as with

rumor or an all but
opaque stone's glow, a dream of
dwindling afternoon and heat

from the bottom
of deep water.

When will its dragon face surfacing
at the end of the line not
surprise me?  The groggy dead

are not lifting heavy lids to join us,
and the future is an easier
page to read, the recto

beyond the spine, the far bank exposed
against the current, and beyond that
the third bank, the third

page of the open
ledger, which for once
is clear—my finger pressing

it flat—the water, whose
shore the page becomes
above dry weeds, just out of

a lost season's reach.
Lambent and stubborn before
dusk's metal finally lathes and draws

the desert together,
flattened into what draws me
into the one dimension

proffered, the sun sets
and my eyes cannot adjust and
shut until awoken

to follow a voice into a tuft
of weedy stalks—*keep your eye on that hollow
tree at the far bank*—

where now are model homes,
whose timed florescence
shines on kitchen counters, living

rooms' easy chairs on cue,
and through the window, the second ghost
tonight is me, climbing the stairs

to a door where my mother, too
weak to walk, must be carried.
Power lines scaffold the floodlit ether

in every picture window framing us.
She is lighter than I dreamed, than air, than
anything I have ever held in

my arms, and it's hard not to
keep lifting her and not rise together
through no one's

furnished rooms
above the unlivable rises
and look down upon the glistening

holes, the artificial lakes,
their shallows
so still even water

is waiting for the word.
Umbra of no one listening,
light of no one in the kitchen.

You will never die,
model homes tell us, halo,
unguent, promise, balm,

supernal-supernatant, no
one ever dies—
festooned by flags:  WELCOME

HOME—*follow me boy*
*there's something you need*
*to see.*

Waterline low in late summer,
the broadcast of experts grows
convincing in the glow,

their lips pressed against our ears,
at eleven years old,
at fifty, their worries are

well-founded, their warnings
bid the eye to wander into cat-claw
acacia, into the reeds,

into the pungent corner spilling dusk
and the flutter of moths,
and who can remember which

conflict they speak of, but
the war is closer, the night air
pressed upon our eyes, the swelling

borders, the experts worry.
Our boarders.

Tall enough to make us wonder what
might live inside their clasping
bases, horned stalks and

chambers, the plexus of
camphorweed pushes through
clay flats along the shores

of the reservoir, a bowl for
what was planned, then built, filled
then spent—*boy, shine it there—*

to be this torn throat
nightfall—*stop shaking, see
its eyes there in the reeds?*

*No? Look hard it's
there.*

Seed-heads, barbed,
held windless by sharp in-
folding, as optic cups

form farthest from light
in the earliest stages of the eye,
ovarian, never dormant to

what takes its time stirring, to
false resemblances we can no longer
court—*there, I see it*

and for which we are
forever marked—*hold it there*
tumult triggered into breath,

startled lift, the no-matter-
how-much anticipated owl
breaking through stalks, whose

wings draw out, fledgling, umbra
of no one, light of
no one, whose wing draws us in.

Notes

1. The opening epigraph is from César Vallejo's *Trilce*, LXIV, translated by Clayton Eshleman.

> *Oh valle sin altura madre, donde todo duerme horrible mediatinta, sin ríos frescos, sin entradas de amor. Oh voces y ciudades que pasan cabalgando en un dedo tendido que señala a calva Unidad.*

from *The Complete Poetry, César Vallejo*, Edited and translated by Clayton Eshleman, University of California Press, 2007.


2. The second epigraph is from René Char's *Le Nu perdu*, the poem "*Effacement du peuplier*," translated by Nancy Kline.

> *Une clé sera ma demeure,*
> *Feinte d'un feu que le coeur certifie;*
> *Et l'air qui la tint dans ses serres.*

from *The Selected Poems of René Char*, edited by Mary Ann Caws and Tina Jolas, New Directions, 1992.


3. "Too Easy Questions on Lonely Roads"
Title taken from W. H. Auden's "Taller To-day."

> Nights come bringing the snow, and the dead howl
>
> Under headlands in their windy dwelling
>
> Because the Adversary put too easy questions
>
> On lonely roads.

from *Collected Poems*, Edited by Edward Mendelson. Vintage International, 1991.

4. "Key"
"Just a door ajar that oceans are..." taken from Emily Dickinson's "I cannot live with You—" #640's final stanza.

> So We must meet apart—
>
> You there—I—here—
>
> With just the Door ajar
>
> That Oceans are—and Prayer—
>
> And that White Sustenance—
>
> Despair—

from *The Complete Poems of Emily Dickinson*, Edited by Thomas H. Johnson, Little, Brown.

As if the key/"may at pleasure join that which nature hath severed..." taken from Francis Bacon's *The Advancement of Learning, Book 2*, Chapter 4.

> I. Poesy is a part of learning in measure of words for the most part restrained, but in all other points extremely licensed, and doth truly refer to the imagination; which, being not tied to the laws of matter, may at pleasure join that which nature hath severed, and sever that which nature hath joined, and so make unlawful matches and divorces of things; "*Pictoriabus atque poetis*," &c.

CPSIA information can be obtained at www.ICGtesting.com
263665BV00002B/43-92/P

9 781936 671014